THE WILD BRAID

ALSO BY STANLEY KUNITZ

At my touch the wild
braid of creation
trembles.

—"The Snakes of September"

* * *

I associate the garden with the whole experience of being alive,
and so, there is nothing in the range of human experience
that is separate from what the garden can signify
in its eagerness and its insistence,
and in its driving energy to live—to grow, to bear fruit.

* * *

The universe is a continuous web.
Touch it at any point and the whole web quivers.

W · W · NORTON & COMPANY · NEW YORK · LONDON

THE WILD BRAID

A POET REFLECTS ON A
CENTURY IN THE GARDEN

STANLEY KUNITZ

WITH GENINE LENTINE

PHOTOGRAPHS BY
MARNIE CRAWFORD SAMUELSON

For information about permission to reproduce selections from this book, write to Permissions, W. W. Norton & Company, Inc., 500 Fifth Avenue, New York, NY 10110

R R Donnelley Shenzhen
Book design by Antonina Krass
Production manager: Andrew Marasia

Library of Congress Cataloging-in-Publication Data

Kunitz, Stanley, date.
The wild braid : a poet reflects on a century in the garden / Stanley Kunitz ; with Genine Lentine ; photographs by Marnie Crawford Samuelson.—1st ed.
p. cm.
Includes bibliographical references.
ISBN 0-393-06141-8 (hardcover)
1. Kunitz, Stanley, date.—Interviews. 2. Poets, American—20th century—Interviews. 3. Gardeners—United States—Interviews. 4. Poetry—Authorship. 5. Gardening. I. Lentine, Genine. II. Title.
PS3521.U7Z478 2005
811'.52—dc22

2005006669

ISBN 978-0-393-32997-1 pbk.

W. W. Norton & Company, Inc.
500 Fifth Avenue, New York, N.Y. 10110
www.wwnorton.com

W. W. Norton & Company Ltd.
15 Carlisle Street, London WID 3BS

5 6 7 8 9 0

CONTENTS

This book grows out of conversations between Stanley Kunitz and myself that began in the summer of 2002 and continued into the fall of 2004. Our talks occurred on daily rounds in Stanley's seaside garden in Provincetown, during afternoons by the harbor, and in New York, in his study, with its lustrous green parquet floor. The prose reflections gathered here are distilled from these explorations, which most often began with gardening and from there wove through such topics as personal history, poetry, the creative process, and the life cycle. In some cases we have chosen to present the material in its original dialogue form.

In the spring of 2003, Stanley experienced a near-fatal health crisis from which he emerged in what he describes as a transformed state. Throughout this period, it was often his vision of the garden that propelled him forward. "Clear my calendar," he told me on his first morning in the hospital. "All I want to do is write poems and be in the garden." That summer, he was, in fact, able to return to the garden, and with a great deal of vitality and clarity of intention. The theme of regeneration was central to our discussions during those months.

In the spring of 2004, Stanley's wife of forty-seven years, the poet and painter Elise Asher, died. In the months that followed, Stanley returned to Provincetown, where again his garden was a source of solace and renewal. Stanley greeted the publication of this book in 2005—just in time for his one hundredth birthday—with "a particular joy." At celebratory events in New York and Provincetown, he gave readings of extraordinary power, embodying his conviction that "poetry is for the sake of life." Stanley Kunitz died on May 14, 2006, at his home in New York.

—Genine Lentine
Provincetown
January 2007

TURNING *the* SOIL

I can scarcely wait till tomorrow

when a new life begins for me,

as it does each day,

as it does each day.

—"The Round"

W|hy is the act of cultivating so compelling?

All my life, the garden has been a great teacher in everything I cherish. As a child, I dreamed of a world that was loving, that was open to all kinds of experience, where there was no prejudice, no hatred, no fear. The garden was a world that depended on care and nourishment. And it was an interplay of forces; as much as I responded to the garden, the garden, in turn, responded to my touch, my presence.

The garden isn't, at its best, designed for admiration or praise; it leads to an appreciation of the natural universe, and to a meditation on the connection between the self and the rest of the natural universe. And this can come not only from the single flower in its extravagant beauty, but in the consideration of the harmony established among all aspects of the garden's form.

The garden is a domestication of the wild, taking what can be random, and, to a degree, ordering it so that it is not merely a transference from the wild, but still retains the elements that make each plant shine in its natural habitat.

In the beginning, a garden holds infinite possibilities. What sense of its nature, or its kingdom, is it going to convey? It represents a selection, not only of whatever individual plants we consider to be beautiful, but also a synthesis that creates a new kind of beauty, that of a complex and multiple world. What you plant in your garden reflects your own sensibility, your concept of beauty, your sense of form. Every true garden is an imaginative construct, after all.

I think of gardening as an extension of one's own being, something as deeply personal and intimate as writing a poem. The difference is that the garden is alive and it is created to endure just the way a human being comes into the world and lives, suffers, enjoys, and is mortal. The lifespan of a flowering plant can be so short, so abbreviated by the changing of the seasons, it seems to be a compressed parable of the human experience.

The garden is, in a sense, the cosmos in miniature, a condensation of the world that is open to your senses. It doesn't end at the limits of your own parcel of land, or your own state, or your own nation. Every cultivated plot of ground is symbolic of the surprises and ramifications of life itself in all its varied forms, including the human.

Is the cycle any easier to accept in the garden than in a human life? Both of them are hard to take! In both cases there is a sense not only of obligation, but of devotion.

You might say, as well, that the garden is a metaphor for the poems you write in a lifetime and give to the world in the hope that these poems you have lived through will be equivalent to the flower that takes root in the soil and becomes part of the landscape. If you're lucky, that happens with some of the poems you create, while others pass the way of so many plants you set into the garden, or grow from seed: they emerge and give pleasure for a season and then vanish.

WOODS, FIELDS, FARMS

I stood on the rim of the buggy wheel

and raised my enchanter's wand,

with its tip of orange flame,

to the gas mantles in their cages,

touching them, one by one,

till the whole countryside bloomed.

—"Lamplighter: 1914"

W hen I was a child I haunted the woods. The two essential compo-nents of my imagination were my fascination with the natural world and with language.

I loved especially the *sounds* of words. We were fortunate in our house to have an unabridged dictionary. I explored it every day for new words and then I would go out into the woods behind our house and shout my latest discovery and listen to it reverberate. I considered it my duty to give my new words to the elements, to scatter them. The woods were the perfect audience.

I yearned to be lost in another atmosphere, and in history itself, as these woods had the virtue of being one of the encampments of Massas-soit's tribe so I looked out for traces of them. Otherwise, I had no human company, but there were wild animals who soon learned that I was not there to harm them and so I felt I was in a world of friends.

"unburdened by a body"

During my adolescence, out in the open fields, I would sometimes pretend I was one of the insects. I became captivated by dragonflies and imagined I could see the world as they did. Everything had a different scale.

I reveled in the sensation of being so light and being able to go any-where, unburdened by a body.

Discovering the body was part of the joy, the sense of infinite possibility of being out in the woods. I recognized that it had weight and had certain limitations—there was no denying that. Obviously one's sensitivity was less acute than that of any other living creature in the woods. At the same time, the body was the very instrument of exploration.

I would find a leaf or a stone in the underbrush and have the sensation that nobody else had seen quite the same thing. And if I came across an arrowhead, that was a real triumph.

Sometimes, especially when one gets older, one gets very clumsy in the handling of delicate objects. The hands, the fingers, are less nimble than they were. But then, there's the compensation that one knows a bit more. There's a quid pro quo.

In the woods, one loses the sense of time. It's quite a different experience from walking in the streets. The streets are human creations. In the woods what one finds are cosmic creations.

Some of my central poems have their source in the many summers I spent on the Buteau family farm, in Quinnapoxet. I was sent there largely because I was what they called "a delicate child" and the doctor had warned my mother that I was a candidate for tuberculosis and so should get plenty of fresh air and sunlight. I was subject to colds and caught every child's disease you could think of, including scarlet fever.

The Buteau farm was a truck farm. They grew all the staples, and of course they had pigs and cows and horses. One of my duties, though I hardly counted it as one, was to go out into the fields in the evening with the beautiful shepherd dogs to bring in the cows. The shepherd dogs were quite different from domestic dogs I had known. They belonged to the open fields and they relished their job. I loved the way they would scatter, then close in, circling the herd, adroitly guiding them back to the barn.

On the Buteau farm, out in open territory, I was a transformed character, in some respects, more *myself.* It was such a different environment from home, which I felt was too enclosed a world, a house of sorrows. At home, the shadow of my father's suicide loomed over my family. Death was something that stood stagnated in its silence. My experiences on the farm helped me understand death as part of a natural cycle.

THE PORTRAIT

My mother never forgave my father
for killing himself,
especially at such an awkward time
and in a public park,
that spring
when I was waiting to be born.
She locked his name
in her deepest cabinet
and would not let him out,
though I could hear him thumping.
When I came down from the attic
with the pastel portrait in my hand
of a long-lipped stranger
with a brave mustache
and deep brown level eyes,
she ripped it into shreds
without a single word
and slapped me hard.
In my sixty-fourth year
I can feel my cheek
still burning.

At home in Worcester, I found solace in solitude, exploring the realms of the imagination. On the Buteau farm, I was a part of the farming operation.

Quinnapoxet was a small village, maybe two hundred people. The Buteaus had the concession for lamplighting, and I thrilled at the chance to go out on the buggy with Charlie, one of the Buteau sons, and his horse, Prince.

As time went on, Charlie trusted me to go out on my own. It gave me the feeling that I was really a man—my first job. The first lesson I learned was to listen to Prince. He was my mentor. I needed no map, relying instead on his knowledge, on all he had learned as part of his ministry. There were about twenty lamps and I went out every night as twilight was falling. It took me about an hour and a half to travel the whole route and come back.

My job as lamplighter gave me a completely different sense of function. I was a public person—at age nine! But I never thought of myself as being just nine years old.

The time I spent in Quinnapoxet was absolutely right for me. I learned so much about the natural world, about my place in it. One of my very earliest memories of snakes comes from the Buteau farm. I was out scuffing around on a dirt road and looked down and saw my shoelace had come loose so I crouched down to tie it and it wriggled in my hand! It was a little shoestring snake and I'm certain it was every bit as startled as I was.

LAMPLIGHTER: 1914

What I remember most was not
the incident at Sarajevo,
but the first flying steamkettle
puffing round the bend,
churning up the dirt
between the rocky pastures
as it came riding high
on its red wheels
in a blare of shining brass;
and my bay stallion snorting,
rearing in fright, bolting,
leaving me sprawled on the ground;
and our buggy
careening out of sight,
those loose reins dangling,
racing toward its rendezvous
with Hammond's stone wall
in an explosion of wood and flesh,
the crack of smashed cannon bones.
Who are these strangers
sprung out of the fields?
It is my friend, almost my brother,
who points a gun
to the crooked head.

Once I was a lamplighter
on the Quinnapoxet roads,
making the rounds with Prince,
who was older than I and knew
by heart each of our stations,
needing no whoa of command
nor a tug at his bridle.
That was the summer I practiced
sleight-of-hand and fell asleep
over my picture-books of magic.
Toward dusk, at crossings
and at farmhouse gates,
under the solitary iron trees
I stood on the rim of the buggy wheel
and raised my enchanter's wand,
with its tip of orange flame,
to the gas mantles in their cages,
touching them, one by one,
till the whole countryside bloomed.

Toward the end of my summers in Quinnapoxet, my mother married again. Mark Dine, my new father, had a dignity about him that was impressive to me, and great kindness and gentleness. The whole climate of the household changed when she brought in this beautiful man, whose love, above all, saved me from bitterness, which, in the end, would have destroyed me creatively.

During the holiday season in 1918 I had gone to stay with his son Mitchell in Cambridge. One night there was a big demonstration in the streets below the apartment, with fireworks going off until late in the evening, and I had finally fallen asleep well after midnight. Around 3 A.M. the phone rang. I heard Mitchell pick it up and knew immediately something tragic had happened. Mark, my new father, had died of a heart attack.

MY MOTHER'S PEARS

Plump, green-gold, Worcester's pride,
    transported through autumn skies
        in a box marked HANDLE WITH CARE

sleep eighteen Bartlett pears,
    hand-picked and polished and packed
        for deposit at my door,

each in its crinkled nest
    with a stub of stem attached
        and a single bright leaf like a flag.

A smaller than usual crop,
    but still enough to share with me,
        as always at harvest time.

Those strangers are my friends
    whose kindness blesses the house
        my mother built at the edge of town

beyond the last trolley-stop
    when the century was young, and she
        proposed, for her children's sake,

to marry again, not knowing how soon
       the windows would grow dark
             and the velvet drapes come down.

Rubble accumulates in the yard,
       workmen are hammering on the roof,
             I am standing knee-deep in dirt

with a shovel in my hand.
       Mother has wrapped a kerchief round her head,
             her glasses glint in the sun.

When my sisters appear on the scene,
       gangly and softly tittering,
             she waves them back into the house

to fetch us pails of water,
       and they skip out of our sight
             in their matching middy blouses.

I summon up all my strength
       to set the pear tree in the ground,
             unwinding its burlap shroud.

It is taller than I. "Make room
       for the roots!" my mother cries,
             "Dig the hole deeper."

In the early 1930s, in the midst of the great Depression, after living in New York for two years, I left the city because I hungered to be in the country. And I found, in Connecticut, near Mansfield Center, a place called Wormwood Hill, a hundred-acre farm with an eighteenth-century, fifteen-room gambrel house in deplorable condition. It had no convenience of any kind: no running water, no electricity, no telephone, nothing. But I needed very much to live in the country, and so for three thousand dollars—five hundred down—I bought it and spent about three years bringing it up to livable condition.

The woods behind the house were deep and long, and every day I went out and explored them, evoking images of my childhood.

One day, as I stood under a great chestnut tree deep in the center of the woods, I heard some rustling in the branches. I looked up and saw a family of owls, a mother and four fledglings, all on one branch. The moment I moved, they frantically whisked off.

I vowed I would become a friend of theirs, and realized I must not disturb them in any way. I learned if I approached very quietly, advancing just a few steps, then standing still, then advancing a little more, the owls were not intimidated. And then I would reach the chestnut tree and stand under it absolutely motionless for as long as I could, fifteen minutes, half an hour or so.

After doing this day after day for several weeks, I could tell the owls had gained confidence in my presence. Gradually, I dared to raise my arm and lift one of the four babies off its perch and place it on my shoulder for a few minutes and then return it safely. I did that with all of them over a period of weeks and finally made the great maneuver—I extended my arm and lifted them one by one, all five of them, on to my arm. I started with the most familiar one, the mother owl. And then once she was perched there, the others were happy to join. By then they were familiar with my touch. There was no sense of separation; I was part of their life process.

So, with the mother owl and the four little ones perched on my arm I walked gingerly out of the woods and took them home and installed them in the attic where I'd prepared the equivalent of a branch and set out some food to welcome them. They lived there very happily, coming and going through the open window, for the remainder of my stay on Wormwood Hill, until eventually I moved on to another small farm in the town of New Hope in Bucks County, Pennsylvania.

My encounter with this family of owls was one of the most intimate of all my experiences with the animal world, a world I consider to be part of our own world, too.

THE TESTING-TREE

1

On my way home from school
      up tribal Providence Hill
            past the Academy ballpark
where I could never hope to play
      I scuffed in the drainage ditch
            among the sodden seethe of leaves
hunting for perfect stones
      rolled out of glacial time
            into my pitcher's hand;
then sprinted lickety-
      split on my magic Keds
            from a crouching start,
scarcely touching the ground
      with my flying skin
            as I poured it on
for the prize of the mastery
      over that stretch of road,
            with no one no where to deny
when I flung myself down
      that on the given course
            I was the world's fastest human.

2

Around the bend
        that tried to loop me home
                dawdling came natural
across a nettled field
        riddled with rabbit-life
                where the bees sank sugar-wells
in the trunks of the maples
        and a stringy old lilac
                more than two stories tall
blazing with mildew
        remembered a door in the
                long teeth of the woods.
All of it happened slow:
        brushing the stickseed off,
                wading through jewelweed
strangled by angel's hair,
        spotting the print of the deer
                and the red fox's scats.

Once I owned the key
        to an umbrageous trail
                thickened with mosses
where flickering presences
        gave me right of passage
                as I followed in the steps

of straight-backed Massassoit
        soundlessly heel-and-toe
                practicing my Indian walk.

3

Past the abandoned quarry
        where the pale sun bobbed
                in the sump of the granite,
past copperhead ledge,
        where the ferns gave foothold,
                I walked, deliberate,
on to the clearing,
        with the stones in my pocket
                changing to oracles
and my coiled ear tuned
        to the slightest leaf-stir.
                I had kept my appointment.
There I stood in the shadow,
        at fifty measured paces,
                of the inexhaustible oak,
tyrant and target,
        Jehovah of acorns,
                watchtower of the thunders,
that locked King Philip's War
        in its annulated core
                under the cut of my name.

Father wherever you are

I have only three throws

bless my good right arm

In the haze of afternoon,

while the air flowed saffron,

I played my game for keeps—

for love, for poetry,

and for eternal life—

after the trials of summer.

4

In the recurring dream

my mother stands

in her bridal gown

under the burning lilac,

with Bernard Shaw and Bertie

Russell kissing her hands;

the house behind her is in ruins;

she is wearing an owl's face

and makes barking noises.

Her minatory finger points.

I pass through the cardboard doorway

askew in the field

and peer down a well

where an albino walrus huffs.

He has the gentlest eyes.

If the dirt keeps sifting in,
        staining the water yellow,
                why should I be blamed?
Never try to explain.
        That single Model A
                sputtering up the grade
unfurled a highway behind
        where the tanks maneuver,
                revolving their turrets.
In a murderous time
        the heart breaks and breaks
                and lives by breaking.
It is necessary to go
        through dark and deeper dark
                and not to turn.
I am looking for the trail.
        Where is my testing-tree?
                Give me back my stones!

PROVINCETOWN

Let's jump into the car, honey,

and head straight for the Cape,

where the cock on our housetop crows

that the weather's fair,

and my garden waits for me

to coax it into bloom.

—"Route Six"

Early in the 1930s, when I was living on Wormwood Hill, I had been reading about the generation of Eugene O'Neill, Susan Glaspell, and so many others who had been associated with Provincetown very early in the century, and I decided one day to hop in my Model A Ford and drive to Provincetown, out at the very tip of Cape Cod, to have a look and to get the benefit of the sun and the sea.

I arrived late in the afternoon, and on the beach in the center of town, I chanced upon a considerable group of people painting the seascape. They turned out to be students of Charles Hawthorne and there he was, surrounded mostly by women, in their long skirts, most of them wearing sunbonnets. It was a scene out of another age. I was simply fascinated not only by that class on the beach, but by the fishing village, this typical New England town of a kind I had never seen before. The next day I returned to Connecticut, but I knew someday I would be back.

That "someday" was twenty-some years later when Elise Asher and I joined forces and we decided to spend the summer in Provincetown, a place with which she was already familiar. So we did, renting for the summer, right on the beach, a shack that we learned later had been the studio of the painter Blanche Lazelle, which has now been destroyed, and is forever lost—except in memory, and I remember it very well.

We returned every summer after that. Our beach shack became a gathering place for many of our friends, including Mark Rothko, Franz Kline, Robert Motherwell, and others.

What drew me to Provincetown was its cultural history, its reputation, after its literary and fishing origins, as a center for writers, painters, and sculptors. After several years we decided that this would be our summer place and we wanted to buy some property of our own there.

"I began to see a garden."

In 1962, I found the house on Commercial Street in the West End and we decided to purchase it—for one reason: it was so cheap! Also, for a curious other reason—it was in such poor condition, so shabby, I thought I would not be tempted to spend much time transforming it. My plan was to keep the house simple and not have a lot of projects to do. But from the first moment I saw the house, I began to see a garden.

After moving into our new home, we fell in love with it and occupied it together for over forty summers. June 21st was our wedding day and it was also the summer solstice and we felt those were two auspicious reasons for traveling, along with our cat, Celia, to Provincetown on that date each year. We customarily stayed through October, returning often on Halloween.

Fall is a beautiful time in Provincetown. Those great blue skies! And there's a certain fragrance in the air out of the brine and the fallen leaves. It is certainly one of the beautiful spots on earth.

I do not know of a place that is comparable to it, with its vast seascapes, the glorious Cape light, the air that flows in from the sea, and a community of deeply engaged artists. I find the combination of the gardening and the long nighttime hours at my desk to be just the right medicine for my soul.

I have dear friends here, and of course, the Fine Arts Work Center community means a great deal to me. They're all very much a part of my life, as is the juniper at my front door!

I have never missed a summer.

ROUTE SIX

The city squats on my back.
I am heart-sore, stiff-necked,
exasperated. That's why
I slammed the door,
that's why I tell you now,
in every house of marriage
there's room for an interpreter.
Let's jump into the car, honey,
and head straight for the Cape,
where the cock on our housetop crows
that the weather's fair,
and my garden waits for me
to coax it into bloom.
As for those passions left
that flare past understanding,
like bundles of dead letters
out of our previous lives
that amaze us with their fevers,
we can stow them in the rear
along with ziggurats of luggage
and Celia, our transcendental cat,
past-mistress of all languages,
including Hottentot and silence.
We'll drive non-stop till dawn,

and if I grow sleepy at the wheel,
you'll keep me awake by singing
in your bravura Chicago style
Ruth Etting's smoky song,
"Love Me or Leave Me,"
belting out the choices.

Light glazes the eastern sky
over Buzzards Bay.
Celia gyrates upward
like a performing seal,
her glistening nostrils aquiver
to sniff the brine-spiked air.
The last stretch toward home!
Twenty summers roll by.

Nothing had been done at all in the sand dune that was our front yard so I was confronted with a starkly barren area with nothing growing on it, not even grass. There was a precipitous drop of almost fifteen, twenty feet in a space about fifty feet long by thirty-seven feet wide.

The moment I began turning the ground over, the sand started drifting. My main problem was to prevent the whole hill from collapsing so I had to go down to the dump and collect old doors and boards and anything else I could find to create temporary barriers.

That first summer I worked every day, with welcome assistance from willing friends and family. I also got in touch with a mason in Orleans, a young man who advertised himself as someone to build terraces, and that whole summer we worked together. It was a huge job—it took literally a ton of bricks.

We had to keep the sand from swamping the whole enterprise. The yard looked disastrous. People stopped and asked, "What's going on here?"

I realized if I enriched the soil by importing seaweed and peat moss and manure, I could keep it from drifting. To collect the kelp for the beds, I walked along the bay with my rake and bushel bag looking for deposits on the shore. Sometimes I would wait until after a storm, which would usually bring in a great supply.

On average I would come home with about six bags each day, depending on how lucky I was with the seaweed accumulation. If I missed a day, that would hold up work on the terraces because we needed to incorporate the seaweed into the soil in order to build the beds.

We started at the bottom and worked up. We had to have the barriers up to prevent the soil from tumbling down to the bottom of the slope. It took two summers to complete the terraces. Then as we filled in the levels, I planted small shrubs to hold the soil together. Over the first ten years, I kept adding new plants, but the first five to ten summers were devoted to cultivating the garden's adaptability and fertility. I experimented with plants each year to see which would survive and which would be right in each tier and so forth. Even from tier to tier, there can be very different conditions, for example, in the amount of sunlight a plant receives.

The brickwork has held up admirably well. I've had a professional bricklayer come by only once in over forty years to restore areas of the wall that were beginning to crumble or loosen up.

THE MULCH

A man with a leaf in his head
watches an indefatigable gull
dropping a piss-clam on the rocks
to break it open.
Repeat. Repeat.
He is an inlander
who loves the margins of the sea,
and everywhere he goes he carries
a bag of earth on his back.
Why is he down in the tide marsh?
Why is he gathering salt hay
in bushel baskets crammed to his chin?
"It is a blue and northern air,"
he says, as if the shiftings of the sky
had taught him husbandry.
Birthdays for him are when he wakes
and falls into the news of weather.
"Try! Try!" clicks the beetle in his wrist,
his heart is an educated swamp,
and he is mindful of his garden,
which prepares to die.

This garden, just across the street from the harbor beach, is intrinsically connected to the marine environment. It has a different tone, for example, from my Wormwood Hill farm garden, surrounded by woods, or from my garden in New Hope, Pennsylvania, with its flat terrain of fertile black soil and wild persimmons.

Whether I was conscious of it or not, I was thinking of the sea when I was planning this garden. In its design, its fluidity, this garden suggests the sea in many respects. For some forty years now, I've continued enriching the soil with the rockweed gathered from the harbor beach. And the plants, for example the lavender and the roses, all respond positively to the sea air. The successive inclination of the garden gives it an illusion of motion, echoing the changing depths of the sea.

It is imperative for any gardener to respect the land before alterations, modifications, or plans for the design of the garden are made. If a garden doesn't fit into that landscape and reflect it in some way, it's an invasion, an occupation.

Certainly gardening has many collaborative aspects to it. You're helping to create a living poem. Philosophically, the garden is a co-creation; it expresses something of the character of the place itself, something that any human intervening there must respect.

This is one of my principles in teaching as well. It's a terrible mistake to impose your pattern on a student. Something that especially pleases me about my students is that they're all so different, each one. What one needs to cultivate in a young poet is the assertion of that particular spirit, that particular set of memories, that personhood.

The Alberta Spruce

In the first year of my garden, I planted four Alberta spruces, one at each corner. Forty years later, in the summer of 2002, after much anguish, I decided to take out the one occupying the southeast corner. It had grown to twenty feet and dominated the entrance, almost entirely blocking the path.

I watched them cut this magnificent spruce down and as it started to topple it was like watching a house burn. All those years!

Gerard Manley Hopkins's poem "The Binsey Poplars" comes to mind— how desolate he felt at a whole row of poplars going down. Of course, I initiated this, and though I didn't feel guilty, I, too, had a desolate feeling. Removing it seemed a radical and cruel gesture to satisfy my need for ease of entrance, but as a result, the whole lower part of the garden was brighter and more open.

When the time comes for cutting, gathering, moving, removing, one has to be pretty ruthless. It took maybe fifteen minutes for them to cut it down. It came down all in one piece. The root system took longer to hack out than that one decisive cut through the trunk—one can easily sense the metaphorical resonance in that.

This spruce represented for me the rising of the sun, since it always caught the morning light. And, as it was host to a whole family of garden snakes, it became the source of the poem, "The Snakes of September." As each summer approached its end, they got bolder and bolder, dangling from the top of the spruce to the bottom, snugly entwined, as they sought the warmth of the sun. I saw them as "the wild braid of creation."

The snakes had learned they were in no danger, and allowed me to stroke them. What gave me particular satisfaction was that they had become so accustomed to my stroking, they seemed to quiver in a kind of ecstasy.

As the days grew cooler, and the snakes became more and more lethargic, I felt they were actually waiting for me to appear, that it had become part of their ritual of survival. I imagined over the years that this awareness was bred into the family, that they had passed on the news. They usually stopped appearing in mid-October, just before my time of departure.

In the poem, I refer to the snakes as being "co-signers of a covenant." There's something very important to me about having a kind of relationship, with plants and animals, that can be transacted wholly without language. The warmth of one's body is a form of communication. The stroke of one's hand is a means of communication. In the garden those forms are heightened. I have a tendency when I'm walking in the garden to brush the flowers as I go by, anticipating the fragrant eloquence of their response. I get a sense of reciprocity that is very comforting, consoling.

There are forms of communication beyond language that have to do not only with the body, but with the spirit itself, a permeation of one's being. I strongly identify with Henry James when he wrote, in answer to a letter asking him what compelled him to write, "The port from which I set out was, I think, that of the essential loneliness of my life. . . ." One of the great satisfactions of the human spirit is to feel that one's family extends across the borders of the species and belongs to everything that lives. I feel I'm not only sharing the planet, but also sharing my life, as one does with a domestic animal. Certainly this is one of the great joys of living in this garden.

THE SNAKES OF SEPTEMBER

All summer I heard them
rustling in the shrubbery,
outracing me from tier
to tier in my garden,
a whisper among the viburnums,
a signal flashed from the hedgerow,
a shadow pulsing
in the barberry thicket.
Now that the nights are chill
and the annuals spent,
I should have thought them gone,
in a torpor of blood
slipped to the nether world
before the sickle frost.
Not so. In the deceptive balm
of noon, as if defiant of the curse
that spoiled another garden,
these two appear on show
through a narrow slit
in the dense green brocade
of a north-country spruce,
dangling head-down, entwined
in a brazen love-knot.
I put out my hand and stroke

the fine, dry grit of their skins.
After all,
we are partners in this land,
co-signers of a covenant.
At my touch the wild
braid of creation
trembles.

The juniper was among the first trees I put in and it took to its site very readily. It's planted in an exposed spot and through the successive hurricanes it showed a tendency just to break off, so I decided that instead of encouraging it to grow tall I would prune it and treat it almost as a bonsai tree. There's no doubt that I've been influenced by the art of bonsai. I am interested in scale, and in allusion, so that would be a natural affinity.

I kept pruning it back, converting its battered state into an aesthetic principle, and now it has taken on a completely different shape, spreading rather than growing upright. As with the making of a poem, so much of the effort is to get rid of all the excess, and at the same time be certain you are not ridding the poem of its essence.

The danger is that you cut away the heart of a poem, and are left only with the most ordered and contained element. A certain degree of sprawl is necessary; it should feel as though there's room to maneuver, that you're not trapped in a cell. You must be very careful not to deprive the poem of its wild origin.

Another reason for my treating the juniper with special care is that years ago, especially during the winter, in my absence, the neighborhood children loved to come into the garden to climb and swing on it. It suffered greatly from their affections!

The juniper, with its densely patterned bark and graceful canopy, is quite handsome. It establishes a line between the house and the garden. Part of the design of that end of the garden is to protect the privacy of the house and in fact one is really invisible unless one emerges into the garden. I like that, especially since Commercial Street is such a public street.

In planting the tree so that its branches grew over the stairway, I was conceiving of it as a kind of shelter. It has an inviting quality there, offering a degree of security, that is if you don't bump your head against it. It's a sentinel, a guardian. It's a tough bird, I know, that tree. I feel very kindred with it in that it's come through many manifestations.

The Lamentation Tree

When we first moved in, there was a wild cherry tree, rather nondescript, growing there in a bed of ivy by the cellar door in front of the house. It was the only tree in the garden area, and, like most wild cherry trees, it was infested with gypsy moths and all sorts of destructive creatures. I managed to get rid of most of the visible insects, but the tree showed no signs of recovering and it was clear I was fighting a lost cause in trying to preserve it.

While digging to see what was causing all that devastation, I found that the roots were being devoured by root borers so I tried everything to get rid of them, and meanwhile the wild ivy kept growing. It seemed immune to the insects devouring the tree itself. And soon the ivy covered the whole tree and began dangling from it. In time the tree assumed the character of a woman locked in mourning.

Seeing the tree this way brought me back to my Bennington years, between 1946 and 1949. Martha Graham was there at that time and I was very interested in her work and often watched her classes. I remember in

particular her saying to a group of dancers, "Stop! You all look so self-conscious, and self-consciousness is always ugly!"

She was trying to cultivate in them a sense of fluid movement and at the same time she was interested in far more than anatomical exercises. She tried to convey a sense of the mythological powers of the body.

One of her famous dances was called "Lamentation." She worked with her group of dancers to find a means of expressing lamentation through the postures of the body, centered in a very contracted torso, bending the body into a pattern that seemed to crystallize all the grief within the powers of the body to express without language. Gradually my ivy-burdened cherry tree seemed to take on the exact same posture. It was so bent over with the weight of its grief that it no longer reached toward the sky but toward the earth, and so I named it "The Lamentation Tree."

The ivy continued thriving, becoming heavier and heavier, killing off the last traces of life in the original tree. This was a period of frequent tropical storms and hurricanes late in the season, and the tree no longer seemed capable of resisting these high winds. In the late sixties, at the height of a hurricane that was battering us, the dying branches no longer could sustain its weight and the whole tree gave way.

I remember very well cutting it into pieces—it was rotted all the way through—and getting rid of it. Then the question remained, how was I going to give a new birth to that place? I settled on a Rose of Sharon called "The Bluebird." It seemed symbolic and mythically correct that a bluebird should succeed my lamentation tree, and it still is there and blossoms exuberantly every year.

The lamentation tree was the most conspicuous eccentricity in the garden during those early years. I've always regarded it as an allegory of the capacity for change in nature. That tree changed its character and took on a life of its own, transforming from a wild diseased cherry tree into something else, no longer a tree really, but something emblematic, mythological.

Part of the fascination of gardening is that it is, on the one hand, a practical exercise of the human body and, on the other, a direct participation in the ritual of birth and life and death.

"a concentration of cosmic energy"

Why did I from the beginning want to have the Dawn Redwood, the oldest of all living trees, why did I want that in my garden? Why did I want the Temple Cedar? To me they were correspondences to my own sense of being, with its love for the whole history of the race, and of language—from the very beginning, the accumulation of sense within the syllables of a word, for example. The antiquity of a tree is a concentration of cosmic energy. That's always fascinated me.

"Light splashed . . ."

I've always had a fondness for Japanese anemones. The variety in my garden is called "Queen Charlotte." I've had them in every garden.

They have very upright flower stalks. The buds themselves have a lovely dignity about them. When they're open, they're sturdy and upright, yet delicate at the same time. I'm drawn to their long life; they stay in bloom for weeks upon weeks, and don't suddenly shrivel up.

I admire how the flower head shoots way above the foliage and seems to have an independent spirit of its own. In their compression and, at the same time, fluidity, anemones (from the Greek for "wind") are very closely connected to the seaside nature of this garden, especially in the way they respond to the sea breeze. Their loose formation is beguiling within itself, and still, the flower head is so neatly articulated—it seems almost as though it might be a shell that beaches.

In August the garden enters into its prime period. I love seeing all those anemones in bloom, all the annuals settled and underway. And the Diana, in full flowering, is magnificent in its purity and quite massive. It seems perfect for what it wants to do, which is to shine.

As August comes to a close, my thoughts start to shift toward fall and New York, my schedule and readings and so forth. I never am absent from the garden, even when I'm away from it. It's an abiding companion during the whole year. It's what I think of first when I think of leaving: I think of returning.

"a very sensitive keyboard"

There's a conversation that keeps going on beyond the human level, in many ways, beyond language, extending into the atmosphere itself. Weather is a form of communication. There is an exchange between the self and the atmosphere that sets the tone for an entire day. The changeability, its overwhelming range of possibilities, exercises a more defined influence on human moods than perhaps anything else. There is no weather or promise of weather that is so alien to our inner responsiveness that we cannot match it with a degree of feeling. That's the curious aspect

of it. That's why each morning, the first thing I look at is the sky, and that puts me in tune with the day.

The storm we had the other day was rather spectacular; I felt it was somehow a message. It seemed so threatening at first, and then suddenly it was just a little downpour. And then it dissolved into a quite peaceful late afternoon. I interpret it positively. I had felt a sense of foreboding, certainly for the last few months, and psychologically this seemed to say, "Stop thinking negatively about whatever's happening now. Find out what you can do, and do it."

And the day was dominated by the visit of dear friends. There was a feeling of real harmony, a lifting of spirit, a sense of blessing in the air. It was a good day. A good day.

We have storms and stresses and positive indications and negative indications that affect us every day. Each of us is a very sensitive keyboard.

When the skies are ablaze, it's hard to focus on anything else. We've all been through so many storms, they all seem to merge into a single great storm, lashing across.

In a similar way, when you have an overwhelming emotional or psychological crisis, the taste of it is so full of memories it encompasses the whole history of losses.

The Garden Cycle

Putting the garden to bed entails, first of all, doing the last weeding and then mulching the beds, doing the last trimming. It's an important and decisive time. It brings a sense of completion to one's responsibilities in relation to the garden.

The main obligations of the gardener are to be mindful of the garden's needs and to be observant each day of what is going on in the garden. And it compels you to structure your life because there are things you have to do at certain times.

There is very little fundamental change in the garden from year to year now; it's really a question of preventing the garden from smothering itself, of selectivity, of moving a plant that doesn't seem quite right in its place. Some things get overgrown, or die from a hard freeze, or a plant shades out one next to it—these things are ongoing and you have to respond to them as they happen. And the garden is not deceptive. The garden lets you know.

Compost

The compost pile is a site of transformation, taking what has been cast off and returning it to the garden. It's not just garbage, after all.

The distillation of any philosophy of composting has some connection with the positive concept of waste and death. The contribution that mortality makes to civilization is the equivalent of what composting contributes to a garden.

We are all candidates for composting. So we cannot approach the compost heap without a feeling of connection.

* * *

As I prepare to return to New York for the winter, the garden is saying a hearty "farewell."

Looking at the garden right now is very complicated for me because it's so freighted with memories. And I can't help wondering what's going to happen to it in the years to come. I'd like it simply to continue, that's all.

Mainly it's a question of perpetuating it, keeping it in good condition. It needs no radical changes or integrations. I'd like it to continue basically as it is, as a perennial garden. I don't want it to be an exuberant annuals garden, flashy in any way. I don't want the familiar plants like zinnias, that sort of thing, dominating the garden. In the future, someone might want to introduce some early plants, for example, some spring bulbs.

I don't believe in setting up taboos or restrictions. I trust that anyone with sensitivity to the spirit of the garden will be able to take care of it.

A LIVING POEM

I am not done with my changes.

—"The Layers"

I s it ever possible to have a poem as glorious as this gentian blossom? It would be difficult. I heard someone say once, "I'd rather look at a painting of a sky any day than the sky." I have to say that's one of the more preposterous things I've heard. Sometimes I walk out and see the sky in all its changeability—especially here on the Cape—and recall that statement. It's like saying you'd rather read a love story than be in love.

"an image that flows"

On some level, when I was looking at that sloping sand, I had a vision of my garden as it is now, certainly in terms of its composition, structure, and form.

What I wanted was to heighten the image of a garden that seems to have taken over a steep hillside, something at rest and in motion at the same time.

The colors of flowers have different vibrations, akin to what Rimbaud spoke of when he referred to the colors of vowels. Rimbaud was one of my very early influences, so that would be a natural alliance here in this garden. There is an internal motion, a sense of timing arising out of the nature of this particular garden, of the plants growing and blooming and fading and falling away. And there is the natural motion that comes from the wind itself.

There are so many expressions of what we call "beautiful." The sand dune that was originally there had a beauty of its own, with its reminiscence of the great dunes along the borders of the sea in Provincetown, but this was not suitable for a domesticated situation. The plan was to bring the wild beauty of the dunes into a different context and transform it into a habitat teeming with organic plant life.

When I'm away from the garden, the image I have of it is an image that flows. Mainly I don't picture it as individual plants, but as a multitude.

Stanzas

I conceived of the garden as a poem in stanzas. Each terrace contributes to the garden as a whole in the same way each stanza in a poem has a life of its own, and yet is part of a progressive whole as well.

The form provides some degree of repose, letting our mind rest in the comparatively manageable unit of the stanza, or terrace. Yet there is also a need to move on, to look beyond the stanza, into the poem as a whole.

Often, when you finish reading a poem, the impulse is to revisit the beginning now that you've been all the way through it, and then each subsequent trip through the poem is different and colored by having seen the whole thing.

Once you have perceived the garden as a whole, the individual tiers of the garden take on a different form because you have seen them both as a part and as a whole. One of the mysteries of gardening is that the garden reflects the viewer's own state of being at the time, just as your response to a poem lets you know something about your preoccupations or your susceptibility as you read it.

The garden communicates what it shows to you but you also contribute to the garden some of what you are seeking in terms of your own life, your own state of being. One reason a garden can speak to you is that it is both its own reality and a manifestation of the interior life of the mind that imagined it in the beginning.

The Gate to Hell

In naming the area I call "The Gate to Hell" I was playing on the verbal concept that this was the dead end of the garden. That set up an image that then translated to its being the gate to the underworld. After I started calling it that, it became that in my imagination, and then it became a burial spot. Our cat Celia is buried there.

I don't find it unfriendly, in any way. Actually, my curiosity draws me to it rather than persuades me to stay away. I have an image of labyrinthine caves starting there, and secrets that are kept from anyone here on earth, except in imagination. It seemed just the right place for an underworld passage to start.

It's the area of deepest shade in the garden under the cryptomerium and the yew hedge. The plants that flourish there now—lamium, hostas, ferns, ivy, and the delicate epimediums with their heart-shaped leaves— are what remain from all sorts of experiments in survival. That area has such a different feel from the boisterous second tier, with its cosmos and salvia and roses, all growing in full sun.

The selection of plants in one tier conditions what will go into the others. The rhythm of the garden is a form of motion, actually. The connection between flowers at different levels of the garden makes a bridge between the different parts of the garden, and the eye, in motion, responds. For example, the platycodon below, and the thalictrum in the tier above it, have a definite relationship. They vary in every possible way you can think of, including the size of the flower, but they have a connection in their color. The blues have a strength of character that makes them particularly effective in the planning of the garden. The pinkish blue of the thalictrum is a modification of the deep blue of the platycodon. The eye responds by bridging the space between the two, making a single visionary action that embraces the different tiers of the garden.

And they both have a delicacy and strength. Considering the height of the thalictrum, it's remarkable that they stand so upright. We could say the platycodon is *rhyming* with the thalictrum. Repetition can unify an experience; it's very comforting, reassuring, which brings us back to the stanzaic concept. The garden as a whole is full of plants that echo the plants one first perceives from the bottom tier. It's not only a question of color, but of height, and of contrasting foliage, bearing in mind that no single plant must dominate the area, that there is a harmony. That is a first consideration in the selection of the plants. So while hollyhocks were just right in my farm garden, they were disproportionate here. That's why it's so hard to fit cannas in a garden in this region, even if they look perfectly at home in a more tropical setting. In their grandiose way they are beautiful, but they don't blend in here, they're show-offs. And the garden is not only an ornamental place, but a habitat and a civilization.

In a poem as well, when there is a word or line that calls attention to itself and not to the flow of meaning, this can be deadly. The poem has its own laws about what it can contain and what it needs to exclude. You have to trust the poem. The garden, too, will tell you, usually rather quickly, if you've planted something in the wrong place.

(74

I'm drawn to variegated foliage. It has less density than a monolithic plant and catches the sunlight in a way that a uniformly green leaf does not. It brings a certain degree of surprise. Halfway between a green leaf and a flower, it intimates bloom itself.

There are some gardens, for example, that seem almost stationary because of the repetition of one color. I like a garden that dances; variegation of the leaves and variation in color of the bloom and in texture all keep the garden alive.

There are areas where you want the garden to suggest the variability of the emotional life. Too many gardens I've seen seem to express only one mood or one state of being. There is a dependence, a reliance on the effectiveness, let's say, of a single color, as though it were the only state of being that corresponds with one's concept of the beautiful.

"the underlying song"

In so many instances, the poem is muddied by too much explanation, too much exposure. What one is aiming for is the indication of an energy, or a spirit, below the surface, in the secret vaults of the self, that somehow withers under too much exposition or explanation. That's why I've always believed that so much of the energy of the poem comes from the secrets it folds into what we would call, in a flower, its crown. The height of the beauty of a bloom is its folded state, rather than when it's fully opened. The rose when it is just about ready to unfold is at its most beautiful.

We tend to consider bloom to be the ultimate gift of the garden, but the

structure is just as important. For example, the phlox is beautiful in its mass of foliage, even before the blossoms emerge.

In a poem, the secrets of the poem give it its tension and gift of emerging sense and form, so that it's not always the flowering in the poem and the specific images that make it memorable, but the tensions and physicality, the rhythms, the underlying song.

The high spots of a poem could be said to correspond with the bloom in the garden. But you need the compositional entity in order to convey the weight and force of the poem's motion, of its emerging meaning.

And you need the silence. So much of the power of a poem is in what it doesn't say as much as in what it does say. As when a flower is preparing to bloom, or after it has bloomed, when it is suspending its strengths and its potency and is at rest—or seems to be, its mission to flower and to produce seed having been fulfilled.

There's that sense that unless something's in bloom, nothing is going on; it's dead in the garden. People talk about a plant being "done"—"the salvia's done for the season"—as if blooming is all a plant has to do. That's a complete fallacy and limitation.

There are areas in the garden that are in no way reliant on bloom. For example, in the lower garden, there is a large planting of Sieboldiana hostas. Their broad waves of quilted, glaucous foliage create the effect of water. That's an area that always comforts me. It has a kind of assurance, a sense of well-being.

Hostas can be difficult to work into a garden because they have a tendency toward a kind of pride, a self-assertion that can be offensive. Part of that effect comes from their wide flat leaves, but also they seem so much more physical than other plants, muscular: the heavyweight champions of the garden. I've given them space so they're not interfering with

(77

any other growth there. They've taken over that area and they're so comfortable down there, they're not so concerned with dominating. This is their country.

❧ ❧ ❧

Almost anything you do in the garden, for example weeding, is an effort to create some sort of order out of nature's tendency to run wild. There has to be a certain degree of domestication in a garden. The danger is that you can so tame your garden that it becomes a *thing*. It becomes landscaping.

In a poem, the danger is obvious; there is natural idiom and then there is domesticated language. The difference is apparent immediately when you sense everything has been subjugated, that the poet has tamed the language and the thought process that flows into a poem until it maintains a principle of order but nothing remains to give the poem its tang, its liberty, its force. Once the poem starts flowing, the poet must not try to dictate every syllable.

"never try to explain"

There were no paths; I had to create the paths. There was a question of where they should be. I finally set them along the front because I wanted the view of the garden looking up. It seemed to me the right way of looking at the garden. I wanted a winding path to the steps in front of the house instead of a straight path. I avoided straight lines as much as possible.

(78

One of my principles is never to try to explain what a poem is about. That's a straight line to me. The path to the understanding of the poem is for me always circuitous, it's a winding path, and I think of the garden as being a winding garden. The poem holds its secrets and keeps its tensions by closing out the opportunity to explain. The fact that it is so secret is what makes it so immediately touching and searching. It is not like explanatory prose that tells you exactly what you have to do to work that refrigerator.

Art conceals and reveals at the same time. Part of the concept of the garden is that you never see it all at once. This I got from my understanding of Japanese gardens, that the way to see a garden is by circling it, by walking through it.

You don't see the garden as a whole from any point, but you begin to know it by making a tour around it. Then it becomes a garden in the mind, and you become the instrument that defines it, just as you have to create the wholeness of the poem in your mind. Though you learn the meaning of a poem, the sense of a poem, word by word, in the end what you have is a fusion.

In the poem, there is an impulse that moves from line to line, from image to image, but complete revelation is not achieved until the poem arrives at its terminal point, at which time what has been secret before the poem begins to reveal itself, and you have to really meditate on the poem. It's like someone removing a garment slowly, slowly. What bothers me about so much contemporary poetry is that there is none of that secrecy; it is all exposition, all revelation. I find that to be a diminishing factor.

Poetry is a secret language. It is not the language of the day. It is not the domestic language. It contains within it the secret sources of one's own life energy and life convictions. And it is not immediately translatable. That's why a poet has to accumulate a body of work before we can even understand how to read the poems. If Emily Dickinson had written three or four of those poems—even her best—they would have disappeared, but there is a life there and it is embodied in that language.

* * *

Thinking of a new season in the garden feels different from imagining a new poem. The garden has achieved its form; it doesn't have to be new each year. What it has to do is grow. You're not going to uproot the entire garden and start all over. The poem is always a new creation and aspires to a transcendence that is beyond telling at the moment when you're working on it. You know you are moving into an area you've never explored before and there is a great difference.

* * *

I wonder if those birds ever tire of their song—I wonder whether a bird ever thinks, "Today I'll try a new song."

THE LAYERS

I have walked through many lives,
some of them my own,
and I am not who I was,
though some principle of being
abides, from which I struggle
not to stray.
When I look behind,
as I am compelled to look
before I can gather strength
to proceed on my journey,
I see the milestones dwindling
toward the horizon
and the slow fires trailing
from the abandoned camp-sites,
over which scavenger angels
wheel on heavy wings.
Oh, I have made myself a tribe
out of my true affections,
and my tribe is scattered!
How shall the heart be reconciled
to its feast of losses?
In a rising wind
the manic dust of my friends,
those who fell along the way,

bitterly stings my face.
Yet I turn, I turn,
exulting somewhat,
with my will intact to go
wherever I need to go,
and every stone on the road
precious to me.
In my darkest night,
when the moon was covered
and I roamed through wreckage,
a nimbus-clouded voice
directed me:
"Live in the layers,
not on the litter."
Though I lack the art
to decipher it,
no doubt the next chapter
in my book of transformations
is already written.
I am not done with my changes.

assonance + consonance

THE WILDERNESS

To be like Orpheus, who could talk

with animals in their own language:

in sleep I had that art, but now

I've waked into the separate

wilderness of age,

where the old, libidinous beasts

assume familiar shapes,

pretending to be tamed.

—"Raccoon Journal"

O ne of the great delights of poetry is that when you're really functioning, you're tapping the unconscious in a way that is distinct from the ordinary, the customary, use of the mind in daily life. You're somehow cracking the shell separating you from the unknown.

There's no formula for accessing the unconscious. The more you enter into the unconscious life, the more you believe in its existence and know it walks with you, the more available it becomes and the doors open faster and longer. It learns you are a friendly host. It manifests itself instead of hiding from your tyrannical presence, intruding on your daily routines, accommodations, domestications.

The unconscious is very much akin to what, in other frameworks, I call *wilderness.* And it's very much like the wilderness in that its beasts are not within our control. It resists the forms, the limits, the restraints, that civilization itself imposes. I've always felt, even as a child, that there was the decorum of the social structure, the family structure, and so forth, and then there was the wild permissiveness of the inner life. I learned I could go anywhere in my inner life.

One function of dreams is to inform us that the boundaries of experience are infinitely open and that the limits we perceive in our daily life are in themselves an illusion, that actually to be alive is to occupy territories beyond those we recognize as our physical universe. Each person's dream-life is in itself a universe, a product of a single tangle of membranes and nerve centers and the rest of it. In the dream you move beyond that dominion into one where the rules have not yet been discovered and never will be.

Pressures from the social structure enter into the whole process of wrestling the poem into being. The challenge is not to be intimidated by convention.

I have often said, "I want to perfect my craft so I won't have to tell lies." So often, when you're stumped, the temptation is just to back down, but when you feel *this is so complicated* or *so tenuous* that there's no way you can say it, you have to persuade yourself you *can* say it, that there *is* a way of saying it, that there's nothing that is unsayable. And this gives you strength for the next time.

The poem, by its very nature, holds the possibility of revelation, and revelation doesn't come easy. You have to fight for it. There is that moment when you suddenly open a door and enter into the room of the unspeakable. Then you know you're really perking.

After you've written a poem and you feel you've said something that was previously unspeakable, there's a tremendous sense of being blessed.

There's a sense of emancipation, and then the recognition that you are not absolutely free, that there are limits, restraints, conventions that are the expression of the social order. You recognize that language itself is a creation of the social order; within such limits you travel as far as possible, but your feet are slipping off the roadway into the weeds and the mire.

That's part of the journey. When Hopkins wrote, in "Inversnaid," "Long live the weeds and the wilderness yet," that's exactly what he was saying. When people say they are moved by a poem, they are saying that they have been in touch with the untouchable.

The mystery of the creative process is that the poem is there but *not* there within you, accumulating experience, accumulating images. It needs to be released, but sometimes there are barriers. The poem incites fear; you are coming into truth in the writing of the poem, you are hesitant to explore unfamiliar areas.

If the terrain were familiar, the poem would be dead on birth. I've written somewhere that the path of the poem is through the unknown and even the unknowable, toward something for which you can find a language.

It is that struggle, of course, that gives the poem its tension. If the poem moved only through the familiar, it would be so relaxed that it would have no tension, no mystery, nothing that could even approximate revelation, which is the ultimate goal of the poem.

I've been grounded all my life to believe in the mystery of existence itself. Can there be any possibility of completely understanding who we are and why we're here or where we are going?

These are questions that can never be answered completely so you have to keep on asking, and in some strange way every poem that you write impinges on that mystery. If it doesn't, you really shouldn't write it because it's not really yours. That's why I get angry and impatient with poets who use the medium just to write something pleasant or ornamental or amusing.

• • •

> My garden, my life, my poems—
> a planned disorder
> —*undated journal entry*

July 14

rac-coon, n. from the American Indian (Algonquian)
arahkunem, "he scratches with the hands."

—*New World Dictionary*

July 17

They live promiscuously in the woods
above the marsh, snuggling in hollow trees
or rock-piled hillside dens,
from which they swagger in dead of night,
nosy, precocious, bushy-tailed,
to inspect their properties in town.

At every house they drop a calling card,
doorstep deposits of soft reddish scats
and heavy sprays of territorial scent
that on damp mornings mixes with the dew.

August 21–26

I've seen them, under the streetlight,
paddling up the lane,
five pelts in single file,
halting in unison to topple

a garbage can and gorge
on lobster shells and fish heads
or scattered parts of chicken.
Last year my neighbor's dog,
a full-grown Labrador retriever,
chased a grizzly old codger
into the tidal basin,
where shaggy arms reached up
from the ooze to embrace him,
dragging his muzzle under
until at length he drowned.

There's nobody left this side
of Gull Hill to tangle
with them, certainly not
my superannuated cat,
domesticated out of nature,
who stretches by the stove
and puts on a show of bristling.
She does that even when mice
go racing round the kitchen.
We seem to be two of a kind,
though that's not to say I'm happy
paying my vegetable tithe
over and over
out of summer's bounty
to feed omnivorous appetites,
or listening to the scratch of prowlers

from the fragrant terraces, as they
dig-dig-dig, because they're mad
for bonemeal, uprooting plants and bulbs,
whole clumps, squirming and dank,
wherever they catch a whiff
of buried angel dust.

October 31

To be like Orpheus, who could talk
with animals in their own language:
in sleep I had that art, but now
I've waked into the separate
wilderness of age,
where the old, libidinous beasts
assume familiar shapes,
pretending to be tamed.

Raccoons! I can hear them
confabulating on the porch,
half-churring, half-growling,
bubbling to a manic hoot
that curdles the night-air.
Something out there appalls.
On the back door screen
a heavy furpiece hangs,
spreadeagled, breathing hard,
hooked by prehensile fingers,

with its pointed snout pressing in,
and the dark agates of its bandit eyes
furiously blazing. Behind,
where shadows deepen, burly forms
lumber from side to side
like diminished bears
in a flatfooted shuffle.
They watch me, unafraid.
I know they'll never leave,
they've come to take possession.

THE WEB *of* CREATION

What makes the engine go?
Desire, desire, desire.
The longing for the dance
stirs in the buried life.

—"Touch Me"

T he poet is an anomaly in our culture. The goal of our culture is money and power. And that's not exactly what poetry is about. What *is* it about? That's a hard question. It's about anything the human mind and unconscious can produce. And that's infinite.

Some people may think being a poet is like being, say, a bluebird. It's hardly that. But, then, why not? I wouldn't mind being a bluebird for one day! It certainly would be fun to be perched in my garden, at the top of this spruce here, singing like mad and pursuing another bluebird.

"no maker"

After a certain period, the poem seems to have no maker at all. Poems gather their own momentum and you feel they're moving on their own. You are part of the world in which they are born and come to maturity, but they have an identity beyond the person to whom they are confiding because the poem doesn't really belong to anyone, it belongs to a great tradition. The great tradition includes what I think of as the essential spirit of the poem, which belongs to centuries, and not to any single moment in time.

You cannot know completely what your obligation is in writing the poem. The primary responsibility is to speak the true word and to distill the complexity of sensitivity that enters into any human experience.

The poem becomes a vehicle of this so-called persona or soul, whatever you want to call it; it is a crystallization of your unconscious life. It carries a big load!

The poet doesn't so much disappear into the poem as become the poem. It is a concentration of faculties, of everything you are or hope to be, and at that moment you have a focus not only on your conscious life, but your unconscious world, and it is as much an expression of your whole being as is conceivable.

What one is looking for is what Hopkins calls *the taste of self*, the sense of extraordinary awareness of being, and more than just awareness, responsiveness also, openness. And that is damaged, wiped out by the diurnal—the cares, the responsibilities that each day demand one's attention.

The curious factor is that the day itself cannot be construed as an enemy; it is what gives you the materials you have not only to contend with, but to work with, to build whatever you are capable of building. If you deny the day completely, you're lost.

We have no other world we can actually invade with all our being and at the same time *be* invaded by, so whatever we create is made of the materials of the life. And we should never think of the life as being the enemy of whatever we aspire to create.

•   •   •

When an individual dies, the web connecting all life remains. It is reconstituted. The whole construct is renewed; the individual creatures who inhabit the web keep changing.

And certainly the arts remain as a contribution that lives beyond one's life as the maker of the art, the artist, and if there weren't the continuity of that, then one would have to feel differently about the nature of one's existence.

How could we separate our reading of Hopkins or Yeats or Keats from our sense of the entire human engine itself? The more we understand the poem, the more we understand the body that made that poem. The poem is not just language, it is in itself an incarnation. The poem is more alive than anything except the body itself, and it's less perishable, one hopes, than the body.

When I'm reading Hopkins aloud, I feel I am actually occupying his selfhood and speaking out of it, not simply reciting the words, but somehow merging into his bloodstream and nervous system.

We forget that the human spirit is poured into the art form, and becomes the electric center of that spirit among future populations. You can pick up a poem by Keats or Coleridge and sense the living vibration in the poem. That vibration cannot be removed from the poem. It's a remarkable thing, absolutely remarkable.

Every time we read a poem from the past we resurrect the poet, so that he or she is a presence just as much as anyone living and that's miraculous in itself. Any contribution to civilization is a contribution to immortality and that is why the explorers and the inventors, the artists and the political leaders who contribute to history, to the social structure, are really never gone. That's a most encouraging phenomenon.

"solitary and on its way"

There isn't only one kind of artist in the world, one way of becoming an artist. There is, above all, a need to articulate your own source of being so you will recognize that source and know who you are. How could you be an artist if you didn't explore your own inner life?

There is something in the human being I would call, in the most general terms, a need to transcend the corporeal being and become a person identified by his or her individuating qualities. Every artist I've known has been distinguished, almost from birth, by knowledge of that need to become a self, not just a living body.

As Blake put it, "We must create a system or be enslaved by another man's." You have to practice being yourself, and not merely exist as a number in a world of billions of numbers. Think of, let's say, Hopkins, a complicated human being, intensely aware not only of his inner self but of the world around him, the natural world. It is a blessing he left this record of his presence on this earth.

The creative gift has very complex origins; you're accumulating and digesting experience, trying to discover its meanings, instead of stuffing it into a closet and moving on to whatever happens to you next.

Every experience you have is a lesson in how to live for the next one and if you never learn anything from the experiences of the past, you never mature either as a person or as an artist.

My sense is that you're born with a more or less empty vault. Perhaps the first experiences are even before that, in the womb, and the vault begins to fill with jewels or painful memories. Each memory of a disastrous experience is there, not only as a wound but as a warning. You have to learn how to recognize the return of the same dilemma you've been through before. You have to look at the tag and the price.

Different kinds of memories enter into the making of the self, but among those, there are a few absolutely central memories. They may be traumatic, but they are the crystallization of the creative person's treasure house. Certainly every poet can be identified by the key images that haunt his or her imagination. If you read Keats and Wordsworth in sequence, even though they impinge on each other in many important ways, the identification of any passage in the poems of either one is very clear.

In a sense, all creativity is a process of giving meaning to what is on a universal scale meaningless. The plant and the poet and the gardener collect these disparate, disorganized raindrops, sun rays, passing birds, and make something formal.

Creativity gives form to what in nature is ambiguous, suggestive. Language wasn't there at the beginning. It was created after people had gone through all sorts of experiences and needed to become expressive in order to give meaning to the life.

Paul Celan's formulation that the poem is "solitary and on its way" strikes the ideal balance. A poet needs both the awareness of the self and the desire to know others, to share one's sense of being with others. The poet in the very act of writing the poems is reaching out to others. This search is to find a vessel—to create a vessel first—that will reach others. Art must have a social sense, a sense of the society in which we live and thrash.

As an artist, you are a representative human being—you have to believe that in order to give your life over to that effort to create something of value. You're not doing it only to satisfy your own impulses or needs; there is a social imperative. If you solve your problems and speak of them truly, you are of help to others, that's all. And it becomes a moral obligation.

"saturated with impulse"

So much of the creative life has its source in the erotic. The first impulse is strongly erotic, but then one becomes reflective—a philosophic human being, an explorer—and then as one grows older and older there's a need to renew that energy associated with the erotic impulse.

There is always an element of the erotic in a poem about death. In fact I would venture that all one's feelings about death are a kind of elegy for the erotic, just as all poems about age have that element.

A poet without a strong libido almost inevitably belongs to the weaker category; such a poet can carry off a technical effect with a degree of flourish, but the poem does not embody the dominant emotive element in the life process. The poem has to be saturated with impulse and that means getting down to the very tissue of experience. How can this element be absent from poetry without thinning out the poem?

That is certainly one of the problems when making a poem is thought to be a rational production. The dominance of reason, as in

(103

eighteenth-century poetry, diminished the power of poetry. Reason certainly has a place, but it cannot be dominant. Feeling is far more important in the making of the poem. And the language itself has to be a sensuous instrument; it cannot be a completely rational one. In rhythm and sound, for example, language has the capacity to transcend reason; it's all like erotic play.

That's the nature of aesthetic impulse, aesthetic receptivity. Whether you're walking through the garden or reading a poem, there's a sense of fulfillment. You've gone through a complete chain of experience, changing and communicating with each step and with each line so that you are linked with the phenomenon of time itself. The erotic impulse is so basic to human experience that we can never be free from it, even in old age.

"Desire" is one of the strongest words in the language, which is why, in "Touch Me," as I look back on it, the very sound of that word is like a cry.

* * *

Poetry as a meta medium—
metabolic, metaphoric, metamorphic—
articulating shifts of being, changes
and transfers of energy.
                    —*undated journal entry*

* * *

In the middle of the night, if I wake, as I often do, I hear the sound of the night. Not street noises, or the sounds of animals, a sound of something humming like a motor that seems to emanate from the movement of the spheres.

I hear it very strongly in Provincetown. The night air seems to produce all sorts of secret sounds that simply flow through it and often I'll get up and walk through the house and say, "Where is the sound coming from?" And it's not coming from anywhere in particular; it's a deep pulsing in the universe.

TOUCH ME

Summer is late, my heart.
Words plucked out of the air
some forty years ago
when I was wild with love
and torn almost in two
scatter like leaves this night
of whistling wind and rain.
It is my heart that's late,
it is my song that's flown.
Outdoors all afternoon
under a gunmetal sky
staking my garden down,
I kneeled to the crickets trilling
underfoot as if about
to burst from their crusty shells;
and like a child again
marveled to hear so clear
and brave a music pour
from such a small machine.
What makes the engine go?
Desire, desire, desire.
The longing for the dance
stirs in the buried life.

One season only,

              and it's done.
So let the battered old willow
thrash against the windowpanes
and the house timbers creak.
Darling, do you remember
the man you married? Touch me,
remind me who I am.

RENEWAL

Peace! Peace!

To be rocked by the Infinite!

—"The Long Boat"

March 2003. The following conversation takes place in the Village Nursing Home in New York City on Stanley's third night in this facility after being admitted for rehabilitation following a hospitalization. He is in very fragile condition, moving in and out of consciousness. As we begin the conversation, in an imaginary walk through the garden, Stanley is speaking very slowly and deliberately.

GENINE: Do you want to take a walk in your garden?

STANLEY: Why not? That would be a great thing to do.

GENINE: What do you think is going on in your garden right now?

So, we're at the end of March.

STANLEY: [*pause*] All is stirring. Hope is stirring.

GENINE: I have a feeling you might be having a couple of visitors in your garden at night. The raccoons are probably having a field day in your absence.

STANLEY: Oh. Don't remind me.

[*laughter*]

GENINE: Those rascals. I'm trying to picture what might be blooming.

Oh, I know, you have a lot of scilla.

STANLEY: Mm-hmm.

GENINE: I've seen those bulbs all over the garden and the grassy foliage when we're there in the summer, when the flowers are long gone.

What other animals do you think might be visiting?

STANLEY: Rabbits. Squirrels, of course. The main visitors are the birds.

(113

GENINE: So if we both close our eyes, we can sort of picture sitting on the steps at the street and it's dusk.

STANLEY: Oh. Good.

GENINE: And there's this owl. And there's a nice wind, a light breeze kicking everything up. And I bet you have some small wild tulips in the garden.

STANLEY: Oh yes, always. Strays.

GENINE: Oh, do you know what word I love in the world of random plants?

STANLEY: [*laughs*]

GENINE: That word "sport." When a seed gets blown somewhere, crosses, and creates a different strain, that's called a sport. And it happens a lot in those species tulips. Oh, you know what must be beautiful right now?

STANLEY: What?

GENINE: The hostas.

STANLEY: Oh, yes.

GENINE: They're probably just breaking through the ground. They're probably up a few inches—

STANLEY: Yes.

GENINE: Starting to spread their leaves. That is such a beautiful stage.

STANLEY: I've never had much feeling for hostas; they create a kingdom that's different from any others.

GENINE: The nurse is going to take your temperature now.

[later]

GENINE: We were talking about hostas and you were saying you never had much feeling for them. But you have such a beautiful planting of them. That "pond" area. The sieboldiana. Those beautiful blue ones. You know that area?

STANLEY: Yes. I do.

GENINE: I know what you mean about them, but in your garden they provide a place of rest. [*long pause*] Do you want to try to go to sleep for a while?

STANLEY: I won't be going to sleep for a little while.

GENINE: Okay. So, I'm trying to think of what else. I bet the ferns look really beautiful. I love when they're first coming out of the ground.

STANLEY: Mm-hmm.

GENINE: And they're all curled like that. And you've got all those new plants in the new area.

STANLEY: Mm-hmm.

GENINE: The phloxes. And those different sedums. And that little oak leaf hydrangea.

STANLEY: Mm-hmm.

GENINE: That little tyke.

STANLEY: Mm-hmm.

GENINE: I bet it's looking really good this year. It grew so much in that short period of time after we planted it. It had been in a pot and stayed pretty much the same size, then when we put it in the ground, it practically doubled in about a month. Do you want to try drinking some water?

STANLEY: Maybe so.

GENINE: Dehydrated plant that you are.

STANLEY: [*drinks some water from a straw*]

GENINE: That's great.

STANLEY: [*drinks some more*]

GENINE: This water is what's going to get you to the next step.

STANLEY: It better, or I'll refuse to drink it anymore.

GENINE: Do you want another sip? I understand how you were feeling so sick the last couple of days you didn't want anything. [*long pause*] Do you feel afraid?

STANLEY: What?

GENINE: Do you feel afraid right now?

STANLEY: Afraid? No. No.

GENINE: How do you feel?

STANLEY: I'm just waiting for the next signal to come and I wonder what it's going to be.

GENINE: What do you think is happening?

STANLEY: I think all the forces, all the energies of my life are converging and that I won't know what my destiny is until a compelling voice takes over and it says, "This is the right path for you to go. Follow me." And I'll go.

GENINE: Have you heard that voice before?

STANLEY: Several times, but it becomes more and more compelling each time.

[*later*]

GENINE: What does your body feel like right now?

STANLEY: It looks as though it's inquiring for a home.

GENINE: What kind of home?

STANLEY: A resting place.

(116

[*long pause*]

GENINE: Would you like some water?

STANLEY: Yes.

GENINE: You said earlier your spirit was fighting for possession
of your soul.

STANLEY: It's been that way for some time.

[*later*]

[*Stanley is mostly resting with his eyes closed, but from time to time opens them
and speaks. His facial expression appears concentrated.*]

GENINE: Are you working on something right now?

STANLEY: Yes.

GENINE: What? What are you working on?

STANLEY: A poem.

GENINE: A poem?

STANLEY: Yes.

GENINE: What's in the poem?

STANLEY: It's a poem that says good-bye.

GENINE: What does it say? Tell me more about your poem. What's in it?
What's it made of? [*long pause*] How do you want to say
good-bye, Stanley?

STANLEY: How do I want to do what?

GENINE: You said you wanted to write a poem to say good-bye.

STANLEY: Yes. Well. Let it happen the way it wants to go. That's the way
I always feel about all my poems. I don't want to think about
anything, except to become language. [*sighs deeply*]

(117

GENINE: Are you becoming language?

STANLEY: I had the thought of it, but [*inaudible*]. I don't want to philosophize. All I know is whatever I wanted to do, to say, is through. And that. . . .

[*His breathing deepens and he does not resume speaking.*]

• • •

By the end of this evening, Stanley started to show many of the physical signs of dying and was brought home the following day so he could be more comfortable. There, in the presence of family and friends, he rested, mostly in silence though he was very responsive to those around him, indicating recognition in his facial expressions, or by clasping a hand, sometimes speaking with great effort. On the third day he started to emerge, and within a week he was eating three meals a day and reading *The New York Times* in his favorite chair. He now refers to this period as "when I was in the other world."

Over the spring months, he regained strength steadily. By June, he was able to return to Provincetown.

The garden instructs us in a principle of life and death and renewal. In its rhythms, it offers the closest analogue to the concept of resurrection that is available to us.

I feel I experienced a kind of resurrection and I'm absolutely grateful for having emerged and yet I have no delusions. I've not been promised anything but a period of survival, that's all. There is no pledge of survival beyond that.

I was changing stations, that's it. It was an interesting experiment, but I don't want to repeat it!

"an immortal population"

Life on this planet would be impossible if there were not limits to the span of existence for all living creatures.

In one respect, death is a supporter of life. Just imagine if people didn't die, what kind of world you'd have, the population mounting over the centuries with the oldsters in control—if they didn't weaken to the extent that they were helpless. Think of the problem with food supply and all the rest of it.

From a social point of view, death offers a source of relief in the cycle. From the individual point of view? Well, one really has to have a perspective on human history that recognizes the social disaster that would follow on the creation of an immortal population.

Still, people continue to want immortality—that's personal. But from the standpoint of society itself, there has to be death and birth, and within reasonable terms.

As for my own rumored immortality, well, there are no guarantees. I wish it were true, but it isn't. My recent episode certainly made me feel mortal. But I've always felt mortal.

As a boy, I feared death greatly because I had lived so closely with it within my own family. I never talked to anybody about how I was feeling. I was afraid to fall asleep because I associated sleep with death.

I would read all night. I always had books hidden away I could turn to. I could have read anything—I wasn't looking in the beginning for something great to read—it was just to kill time. That started when I was about seven years old and lasted for a good many years. No doubt that was the beginning of my nocturnal pattern.

There was so much death around me in my family that I had to become reconciled to it or else suffer the consequences psychologically. It was impossible to live with that fear every day, every night.

Only when I understood the contribution of mortality to the history of civilization did I become reconciled to death, not through one specific experience, but from brooding about it. It all may have begun, though, with my mother's slap, when I felt I had to justify death as a positive force. That was the most profound intellectual experience of those years.

It wasn't death itself that was at the heart of my suffering; it was the *fear* of it. I knew I couldn't possibly drive death away; I had to find a rationale. That rationale is fairly simple, that death is absolutely essential for the survival of life itself on the planet; the earth would become full of old wrecks dominating the population, as they would very shortly— civilization would die, that's all.

Can you imagine having your great-great-great-great-great-great-grandfathers and grandmothers tottering around the household? No, death is absolutely essential and that's the hard reality.

When I came to that realization, I felt as if I'd been reborn. And it was purely internal.

THE LONG BOAT

When his boat snapped loose
from its mooring, under
the screaking of the gulls,
he tried at first to wave
to his dear ones on shore,
but in the rolling fog
they had already lost their faces.
Too tired even to choose
between jumping and calling,
somehow he felt absolved and free
of his burdens, those mottoes
stamped on his name-tag:
conscience, ambition, and all
that caring.
He was content to lie down
with the family ghosts
in the slop of his cradle,
buffeted by the storm,
endlessly drifting.
Peace! Peace!
To be rocked by the Infinite!
As if it didn't matter
which way was home;
as if he didn't know
he loved the earth so much
he wanted to stay forever.

GENINE: Do you think what you experienced this spring has any connection to molting?

STANLEY: [*laughs*] What a question!

GENINE: I think it does.

STANLEY: What did I molt?

GENINE: I don't know.

STANLEY: My old self.

GENINE: Does that feel true?

STANLEY: No, I don't think so.

GENINE: *Your old self,* which means what?

STANLEY: What I was before and what I am now?

GENINE: Do you see a big contrast in that?

STANLEY: Yes.

GENINE: How would you describe that contrast?

STANLEY: Well, that knowledge of what I went through and what I survived has given me a sense of . . . bravado. [*laughs*] I can beat anything!

GENINE: Death—That's nothing! You showed a remarkable formal flexibility.

STANLEY: Mm-hmm.

GENINE: I have such a clear impression of your being in a different physical state before and after. Could you talk more about that bravado?

STANLEY: I feel so fortunate in so many ways that I was able to confront the ultimate and somehow move on. It seems miraculous to me.

GENINE: Do you have any idea about how you were able to move on?

STANLEY: No.

GENINE: Any deep instinct about it?

STANLEY: I don't know. I think of the last lines of "The Long Boat" in which I say, "he loved the earth so much / he wanted to stay forever."

GENINE: The bravado you feel now—I know you well enough to know that can't be unalloyed bravado.

STANLEY: No. No. No.

GENINE: What is mixed with the bravado?

STANLEY: Well, I know I'm mortal. [*laughs*] Sooner or later, it will happen. But as long as there is any chance of pulling through, I'll try, that's all. I can't imagine going willingly.

●　●　●

Immortality? It's not anything I'd lose sleep over.

The way I feel now is very encouraging because I have more energy, more determination. I have a sense I'll be around for a while.

As for whether this physical transformation will have an effect on my work, I sense that it will. I'm very eager to get back into the rhythm of work again. I think I'm in the beginning of it. I've been thinking about and talking about the Dark Angel. I have no doubt that will be my next poem.

I feel as though I'm a traveler exploring territory that may not be wholly new, but it has reverberations and images that seem to have a collective presence. It's still a feeling, a sensibility that is mysterious in many ways because I don't know exactly where I am at this moment, in terms of the imaginative, the creative process, but I know I am searching for something different from the terrain I was familiar with. And yet, it isn't simply a new landscape. When I finally come to grips with my night visitor, I'll know more clearly what it is I have in mind, which seems to be a new set of images, but connected very much with my whole history.

I think I'm close to finding out exactly what it is that is going on. I need to work with three or four different manifestations of it, and until I do, I'm still working in a degree of darkness. I've been through an experience that is really a form of revelation and I'm just as curious as anyone about what's going to happen when I come into a writing spell. Something mysterious is happening to me. I'm not quite sure what it is, but I feel quite positive about it.

I've discovered through the years that if I talk about a poem, so much of my energy for the poem goes into the description of the poem that it interferes with the whole process. The surprises should be attached to the process, and the process is internalized, so the more exposed the poem becomes, the more it seems a fait accompli, and there is not as much drive toward realizing it.

When the drive is genuine, it seems to be irrevocable, a deeply erotic process of illumination.

The Dark Angel doesn't bring death with him. He brings with him an aura, an intuition. And his contact with you—I'm trying to find the image for it—is an overbearing weight, you're being smothered. At the same time it's like a cloud passing over you that you engage, and it's combined with exhilaration. You meet your destiny, and there is a sense of being given power at the same time.

It's an inner, inner thing, a realization that you're arriving at an ultimate moment in your destiny, and there's a thrill about that. Destiny is at stake there, and it isn't a question so much of information as intuition. There is that enveloping contact, though, in the wrestling.

I was recently reading Keats's "Ode to a Nightingale" and I had a feeling that maybe this death image can be traced all the way back to Keats.

> Darkling I listen; and for many a time
> I have been half in love with easeful Death,
> Called him soft names and many a mused rhyme,
> To take into the air my quiet breath;
> Now more than ever seems it rich to die,
> To cease upon the midnight with no pain,
> While thou art pouring forth thy soul abroad
> In such an ecstasy!

There's an affinity there to my Dark Angel. As you can gather, it's very hard to define exactly the sense of that weight that is both crushing and freeing. This is beyond knowledge. But the sensation of being visited is very clear. It's happened many times, and always in exactly the same way. It's a transcendent visit, a universal phenomenon, one of those deep images, and that's what makes it so overwhelming.

Your life is reclaimed or yielded—at the same time. You're asked to reckon with something that seeks to stifle you or smother you, and that you have to resist. It may be an image of something inner as much as of something apart from you. But I don't necessarily think they are different. They can be both, at the same time.

I find it very comforting to realize that there is an association with Keats in this, a sense of a shared encounter.

GENINE: How does it feel to be here today?

STANLEY: Ahh, I feel I've gone through a whole transformation. It's like moving into another element, really. In general it's a sense of being in control of your world, and going where you want to go. It's a strange feeling because you have absolute control of your reality and you can make things happen instead of being a prisoner. You're in command of your life and of your spirit, and of your love and everything else. It's the next phase for me of what I went through in my transformation period.

GENINE: Does it involve leaving this body?

STANLEY: Not so much *leaving* it as being in command of it. It's strange. A feeling of power instead of feeling a victim. It's a feeling of being back in control of your life.

For some time now, I've been having dream states that are really like assertions of a life principle, as though I'm defending my life. And I must say this is different from periods when I felt I was losing my life, so it obviously is a manifestation of a new sense of power over destiny itself.

It's more than changing the course of the dream. It's changing the course of your destiny.

It's hard to explain [*laughing*] because it seems, on the face of it, absurd.

GENINE: It doesn't seem absurd to me at all. But I know what you mean.

STANLEY: For a long time, several years, ever since my first illness of this kind happened, I had a sense of moving out of my body. And now I take it as a matter of course. [*lightheartedly*] I can do it! And things happen to me that I had only dreamed of, that's all.

There seems to be a transformation going on in which I have a sense of a new life that I'm possessing. That I am not at all lost. I feel I have found myself, my strength. And I feel in possession of my destiny, not a victim of it. Look at this beautiful day, for example.

GENINE: I know. The day feels completely different from what it was going to be, now that we'll be here another month. It was going to be the last day here. Now it's the first day.

I'm sitting here amazed because sometime last week I started to get an understanding about what I was calling the gross body, gross functions, basic memory, things like that. I was thinking "Okay, so some of Stanley's gross functioning is going on the fritz—"

STANLEY: [*laughter*]

GENINE: So it's amazing to me that you're actually talking in these terms about traveling outside your body. What I was starting to feel was that you were able to navigate a kind of energy that wasn't reliant on what we call a body.

STANLEY: Well, I've begun to feel that way myself. There are so many aspects of being. I feel that for some time now I've been in a sort of control of my body and that it speaks of a power I had not believed in, but it's there and I feel much stronger. I don't know what it represents in physical terms—I've been through so much these last few years, but I don't feel I'm powerless at all.

In these dreams of being lost, uncertain of what is happening, there appears to be a split, as if my consciousness is operating on another level from my body.

Part of the effort is to reconcile the two. One wants above all to have a sense of identity. But it's very fluid.

Behind the sense of who you are—that something is happening and you're aware of what is happening—there is a sense of another level, a state of being that is both yours and not yours.

One simply cannot understand states of being. One can try to interpret them but there is no certainty. I've had these experiences for a long time. It's not as if I'm a stranger to this sense of displacement.

GENINE: So what I'm wondering is: the more you start to see that this kind of awareness outside your body is possible, does that open up any possibility for you about what happens when you die?

STANLEY: Well, it's impossible to separate the two experiences. I think it's a conditioning. And that's why it's always associated with images of being lost.

What we think of as dreams are states of being and they are an awareness of the movement, the passage of your being, part of the change in your reality from a state of being to a state of nonbeing.

I would suppose that awareness gradually dissolves when you die, that's all.

GENINE: *Gradually,* so you think it's even still around for a period after your physical body has died?

STANLEY: Yes. There's no reason to think that the passage of the body from the state of being happens instantaneously. I think it's a gradually dissolving image.

GENINE: So you think it can actually still exist after, say, the heart has stopped and the brain has stopped?

STANLEY: It doesn't mean that you've lost every bit of sensitivity that is inherent in the state of being alive.

GENINE: Yes. That's what I mean by the gross body—the brain, the heart have stopped.

STANLEY: Yes.

GENINE: But then the other capacities are still . . . at large.

[*laughter*]

STANLEY: Yes.

GENINE: Do you think it's possible for that, whatever that is, to then move into another life form? Say, a child who's about to be conceived?

STANLEY: I don't know! [*laughing*] I don't know. Pretty mysterious. But wouldn't it be a big surprise to find you're in another world, and you've assumed another body, and you go out and flourish!

GENINE: Yes! That's an encouraging idea. Does that seem plausible to you?

STANLEY: No!

GENINE: It doesn't?

STANLEY: Well, it'd be nice! I like the idea, but I didn't make this world.

GENINE: Does it seem plausible to you that some little globby couple of cells could meet up with another globby couple of cells and create a whole person?

STANLEY: Whether it is something one can understand is another question. I don't know. My experience with the loss of another, a companion, is that there is a moment when the awareness of the world moves out of the body.

(134

GENINE: You felt that with Elise?

STANLEY: Yes. I could determine that *moment*.

GENINE: What did it feel like? I know it's hard to describe.

STANLEY: Well, there was a sense that there had been a state of passage and it was over.

GENINE: Could you still feel the awareness, but that it had left the body?

STANLEY: Yes. I had a definite sense when it happened. But I knew that the cells of her body were still functioning.

GENINE: So it happened before she medically died?

STANLEY: Yes.

GENINE: How long before?

STANLEY: It was a progressive thing, but it had been going on all that last night.

GENINE: I know exactly what you mean. I've experienced that when I've been with people and animals who are dying. You really can feel it. Where do you think that awareness went?

STANLEY: [*laughs*] Don't ask me.

GENINE: After she medically died, could you feel her awareness around you?

STANLEY: Yes.

GENINE: How would that manifest?

STANLEY: Well, since we were holding hands, it's pretty easy to be expressed in one's hands; in fact it became more and more intense as it finally erupted.

GENINE: Erupted out of her body?

STANLEY: Yes.

GENINE: And then what?

STANLEY: I don't know.

(135

GENINE: In the time following her death, could you feel her presence?

STANLEY: Yes. But there's no proof. It's a function of your body as much as it is of the other's.

GENINE: You mean your body as a receptor?

STANLEY: Yes.

GENINE: Well, really, you say there's no proof, but is there any proof that I'm sitting here with you?

STANLEY: NO! [*laughter*] Goddamn it!

GENINE: Do you ever dream that Elise is with you?

STANLEY: Yes.

GENINE: I know when I have dreams of people who have died, there are some dreams when they're just characters in the dream and they're like anyone else, and I don't necessarily think they're there. In other dreams, there's a very palpable sense of a presence.

STANLEY: Yes. Well, that's what I have. There's a presence and there's an image attached to that presence and it's different from any other experience. It is so much a part of one's own being and yet there is a definite sense of another being. A presence that is as real as anything else, but it's not a physical image, and yet it's definitely there.

GENINE: And you recognize it as her.

STANLEY: Oh, yes. It's very strange. In the dream state, she is always grabbing my hand and it's so real. It's so much a feeling of togetherness. It's really unlike any other experience.

(136

When you look back on a lifetime and think of what has been given to the world by your presence, your fugitive presence, inevitably you think of your art, whatever it may be, as the gift you have made to the world in acknowledgment of the gift you have been given, which is the life itself. And I think the world tends to forget that this is the ultimate significance of the body of work each artist produces. That work is not an expression of the desire for praise or recognition, or prizes, but the deepest manifestation of your gratitude for the gift of life.

THE ROUND

Light splashed this morning
on the shell-pink anemones
swaying on their tall stems;
down blue-spiked veronica
light flowed in rivulets
over the humps of the honeybees;
this morning I saw light kiss
the silk of the roses
in their second flowering,
my late bloomers
flushed with their brandy.
A curious gladness shook me.

So I have shut the doors of my house,
so I have trudged downstairs to my cell,
so I am sitting in semi-dark
hunched over my desk
with nothing for a view
to tempt me
but a bloated compost heap,
steamy old stinkpile,
under my window;
and I pick my notebook up
and I start to read aloud

the still-wet words I scribbled
on the blotted page:
"Light splashed . . ."

I can scarcely wait till tomorrow
when a new life begins for me,
as it does each day,
as it does each day.